Newest titles in the **Explore Your World!** Series

Nomad Press
A division of Nomad Communications
10 9 8 7 6 5 4 3 2 1

This book was manufactured by TC Transcontinental Printing,
Beauceville Québec, Canada
September 2014, Job #67279

ISBN Softcover: 978-1-61930-259-4
ISBN Hardcover: 978-1-61930-285-3

Illustrations by Bryan Stone
Educational Consultant, Marla Conn

Questions regarding the ordering of this book should be addressed to
Nomad Press
2456 Christian St.
White River Junction, VT 05001
www.nomadpress.net

Printed in Canada.

CONTENTS

TIMELINE . . . IV

INTRODUCTION . . . 1
Show Me the Money!

CHAPTER 1 . . . 12
Coins

CHAPTER 2 . . . 28
Bills

CHAPTER 3 . . . 45
Banks

CHAPTER 4 . . . 60
Using Money

CHAPTER 5 . . . 73
Fun With Money

GLOSSARY $ RESOURCES $ INDEX

INTERESTED IN PRIMARY SOURCES?

 Look for this icon. Use a smartphone or tablet app to scan the QR code and explore more about money! If you don't have a QR code scanning device, there is a list of each url in the Resources on page 88.

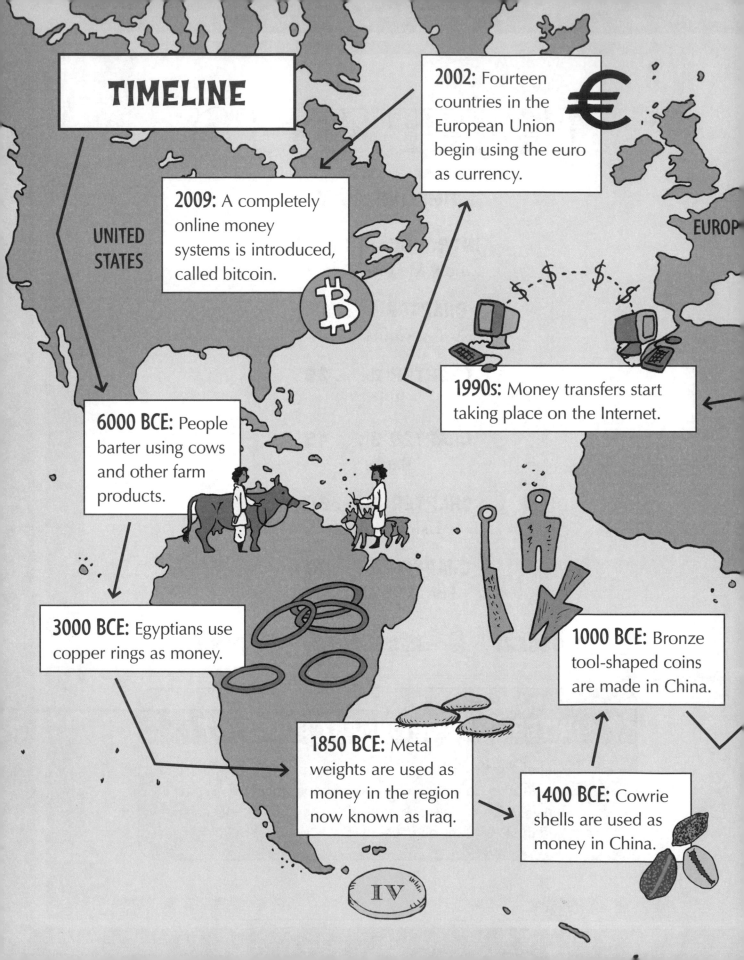

TIMELINE

2002: Fourteen countries in the European Union begin using the euro as currency.

2009: A completely online money systems is introduced, called bitcoin.

UNITED STATES

EUROP

1990s: Money transfers start taking place on the Internet.

6000 BCE: People barter using cows and other farm products.

3000 BCE: Egyptians use copper rings as money.

1000 BCE: Bronze tool-shaped coins are made in China.

1850 BCE: Metal weights are used as money in the region now known as Iraq.

1400 BCE: Cowrie shells are used as money in China.

IV

1971: The U.S. Congress stops backing U.S. currency with gold.

1792: The U.S. Congress establishes the U.S. Mint to make coins backed by gold.

1861: The U.S. Congress passes a law that paper money must be issued by the U.S. government.

1661: Sweden makes the first printed banknote in Europe.

LYDIA

IRAQ

EGYPT

CHINA

1200s: The first handwritten paper receipts are used as money in Europe.

640 BCE: Round metal coins are made in Lydia.

800 CE: The first paper money is printed in China.

550 BCE: The first gold coins are made in Lydia.

What is **money**? Money is those special circles of metal, called **coins**, that jingle in your pocket. Money is also those colorful slips of paper, called **bills**, that you carefully fold and keep safe in your wallet. If you have enough of these coins or bills, you can **buy** something you want, such as a pack of gum, a T-shirt, or a toy. You can also use money to pay for a ride on the bus or a ticket to the zoo.

Where did these coins and bills come from? Why can you use money to buy the things you want, but you can't use a marble or a picture you drew?

WORDS2KNOW!

money: something used to pay for things, including paying people for their work.

coin: a flat piece of metal stamped with its value as money.

bill: a piece of paper money.

buy: to use money to get something you want.

barter: to make an even trade of things that are not alike.

trade: to exchange one thing for something else.

You might wonder how these coins and bills are made and who decides what coins and bills are worth. Can anything else be considered money?

~ BARTERING ~

Before money was invented, people didn't buy things. Instead, they **bartered**. Bartering is a type of trading. The simplest type of **trade** is a swap: "I'll give you my green lollipop for your red one." It's easy when you are trading things that are mostly alike.

But sometimes people trade things that aren't mostly alike. Think about the candy you get on Halloween. Would you swap one piece of gum for one candy bar?

NOW THAT'S BARTERING!

On July 14, 2005, Kyle MacDonald asked people online what they would trade for one red paper clip. The first response he got was an offer for a fish-shaped pen. He went back online and asked what people were willing to trade for the fish-shaped pen. Through the next year, crossing back and forth across North America, he traded up for items such as a camping stove, a snowmobile, and a recording contract. On July 5, 2006, he made his 14th trade for a house in Canada! And it all started with a paper clip!

When trading things that aren't alike, you start bartering. "I'll give you a piece of gum plus a lollipop for your candy bar." Bartering can be simple, as long as there are only a few partners and they are trading small things.

A long time ago, people didn't have money or stores. All they had was what they could find, grow, or make themselves. So they bartered their work and their **goods**.

goods: things for sale or to use.

service: work done by one person for another person.

exchange: to trade one thing for another.

medium of exchange: one item used in all trades.

value: the price or cost of something, what it is worth.

A carpenter might offer a **service**, such as fixing a door, in **exchange** for a blanket. A farmer might barter three chickens for a clay pot. Trading could get complicated. After all, how many carrots would you have to barter for a cow?

～ THE FIRST MONEY ～

Why don't we still barter for everything? Because it can be hard to find people who have what you want and who want what you have. After many hundreds of years of bartering, people began to use other items as their medium of exchange.

Money is a **medium of exchange** issued by a government. It comes in coins made of gold, silver, or other metal. It comes in bills made of paper. Money is used as the measure of the **value** of goods and services.

KNOW YOUR DOUGH

What's the most common medium of exchange at the beach?
Sand dollars!

Just for Fun!

3

preserve: to save food in a way that it won't spoil, so it can be eaten later.

standard of value: an agreement on how much something is worth in a country's medium of exchange.

dissolve: to mix with a liquid and become part of the liquid.

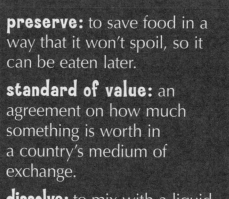

WORDS2KNOW!

In ancient Rome, people used blocks of salt as a medium of exchange. Everyone needed salt to **preserve** and flavor food. Salt blocks could be broken into pieces of different sizes. It could be easily carried around.

People agreed that a certain size block of salt was worth a certain size or number of other things. It had a **standard of value**. A small block could be traded for a piece of meat. A larger block could be traded for new sandals. The cook and the sandal maker could save up their salt blocks and trade them for cows or tools.

Salt was used like money. But it wasn't perfect either. A handful of salt might not be heavy, but large blocks of salt are very heavy and take up a lot of space. What happens if salt gets wet? It **dissolves**! And when you use salt on your food, you have less left to trade.

THAT'LL BE THREE SHAKES, PLEASE.

How did Jack know how many beans to trade for his cow?
He used a *cowculator*!

Just for Fun!

4

People kept experimenting with different items as money. The Sumerians were a group of people who lived more than 5,000 years ago. Today this area is part of Iraq. The Sumerians traveled a lot and they didn't always have the shells, feathers, or tea leaves that were used in other regions for bartering. They started using small bars of silver. It was the first metal money.

A salary is the amount of money a worker is paid each week or month. The word *salary* comes from the Latin word *salarium*, which means salt money. Soldiers in ancient Rome, where they spoke Latin, were paid with blocks of salt.

KNOW YOUR DOUGH

People everywhere liked silver. It didn't dissolve in water, it could be saved to use later, and nobody sprinkled silver on their food! Other countries copied the idea of using metal as money. But the metal bars weren't perfect because they were heavy, yet easy to steal. It was still difficult to make exact trades.

MEDIUM OF EXCHANGE

All around the world, people have used many different items as their mediums of exchange. Some **cultures** have used things that were rare. Other groups of people have used things that were common, but which had no other use. Here are a few mediums of exchange from different places.

* **Rocks with holes**—Yap Islands
* **Blocks of tea leaves**—Tibet
* **Bird feathers**—Vanuatu Island
* **Cocoa beans**—Aztecs in Mexico
* **Whale teeth**—Fiji

5

WORDS2KNOW!

culture: a group of people and their beliefs and way of life.

THE FIRST COINS AND BILLS

BCE: put after a date, BCE stands for Before Common Era and counts years down to zero. CE stands for Common Era and counts years up from zero. The year this book was published is 2014 CE.

Not far away from Sumer was the country of Lydia. This area is now part of Turkey. Around 640 **BCE**, the government in Lydia invented metal coins. It mixed together gold and silver and made each coin the same shape and weight. A lion's head, the mark of the king, was stamped on each coin.

People who had the coins could buy things, whether they had anything to barter or not. This added something new to trading. Coins were much smaller than silver bars. This money could be saved for later because it would not die or rot.

FEATURES OF MONEY

* Money is a way to trade value.
* Money is a medium of exchange.
* People agree how much money is worth.
* Money can be stored or saved.

People around the world copied the idea of using small pieces of metal. The rulers of China didn't have much silver or gold, so they used iron. The problem with iron is that it is a very heavy metal. Then the Chinese invented paper.

When people sold things to **merchants**, they didn't want to carry around a lot of heavy coins. Merchants began giving a piece of paper to a **customer**, called a **receipt**. The receipt showed how many coins the merchant owed the customer. When customers started trading receipts, this was the first paper money!

Today people still barter, but they also use coins, bills, plastic cards, smart phones, and even bitcoins that only exist online! All of these are ways people trade the things they have for the things they want.

merchant: someone who buys and sells goods for a **profit**.

profit: the money made by a business after paying all the costs of the business.

customer: a person or company that buys goods or services.

receipt: written proof that goods or money have been given.

counterfeit: a fake copy made to cheat people.

WORDS2KNOW!

Today members of the U.S. Secret Service protect the president and his family, as well as many other people in the government. But the Secret Service was formed to catch people making and using **counterfeit** money!

KNOW YOUR DOUGH

7

bank: a place where money is kept.

donate: to give something, such as money, food, or clothing, to help others.

invest: to let someone else use your money with the possibility of getting more money back. What you invest in is called an investment.

future: a time that has not happened yet.

~ LET'S LEARN ~ ABOUT MONEY

That's the quick story about money. But there's a lot more to explore! In the following chapters, you'll learn about how money is made, why it's valuable, how **banks** work, and the difference between spending, saving, **donating**, and **investing**.

Did you know there's an easy way to remember how to write and say gigantic numbers? That will come in useful when you create a budget to save your money for expensive items! Take a break from counting to play games with your money, such as flipping paper clips and popping dimes.

You'll look closely at the coins and bills in your pockets and discover that money is valuable not just because you can buy things with it. Money is also a very special way to look at history, the world around you right now, and the **future**.

CREATE YOUR OWN MEDIUM OF EXCHANGE!

Look around your home and yard. What can you use as a medium of exchange? Do you have a lot of pine cones? How about a special type of rock? Does it make more sense to choose items you have lots of or only a few of?

~ ACTIVITY ~
MY MONEY MATTERS JOURNAL

It's important to keep track of your money so you know how much you have. You need to know much you owe, how much you can save, and how much you have to buy the things you want. Adults often keep track of their money on the computer, but you can also use paper. In this activity you'll make a book that will help you keep your money organized.

1 Use the crayons or markers to decorate a sheet of paper to use as your cover. Carefully glue your cover on the front of the binder.

2 Label a divider for each of these:

- My Trades
- Money Math
- Money Facts
- My Savings
- My Spending
- My Sharing
- My **Budget**

3 Put a few sheets of blank paper and a few sheets of lined paper in each section, behind each divider. You will be adding to these sections as you do the activities in this book.

SUPPLIES

- $ crayons or markers
- $ loose leaf blank and lined paper
- $ 3-ring binder
- $ glue
- $ 7 dividers
- $ ruler
- $ pencil
- $ eraser

9

WORDS2KNOW!

budget: a plan for using money.

~ ACTIVITY ~

BARTER CHART

When you barter, you have to decide if one thing is worth as much as another thing. Think of six different kinds of candy. Are they all the same size? Do you like them all equally? What would it take for you trade them?

1 Take a piece of blank paper out of your Money Matters Journal. Use the ruler and pencil to draw a grid that has seven rows and seven columns.

2 Leave the box in the top left corner empty. Draw or glue the wrappers from a different kinds of candy in every box along the top row.

3 Draw or glue each second candy wrapper in every box in the far left column. They should be in the same order that they appear in the top row.

4 Figure out the trading value of each type of candy. For example, would you trade four hard candies for one candy bar? Two Tootsie Rolls for a Blow Pop? Write these values in the correct boxes.

5 When your chart is complete, put it in your Money Matters Journal behind the My Trades tab.

TRY THIS: Try making a barter chart for other things, such as books, baseball cards, or band bracelets. How do your charts compare with charts made by a friend? Do you agree on the values? What would happen if you tried to trade items you disagree on?

SAMPLE CHART

	1	N	2			
		1				
			1			
				1		
					1	
						1

11

COINS

When Sumerian traders began using metal as money, each trader made his own bars of silver. These bars could be traded for blankets, goats, pots, or other goods. People could use the silver bars to buy things they wanted right away or save them to use later.

What was a problem with this system? The silver bars were not all the same. One trader might not accept the silver bars of another trader because they were all different.

Many years later, in nearby Lydia, the government made metal coins that were all the same. These coins could be used by everyone in Lydia. Coins are small, flat pieces of metal made by a government to be used as money. A coin is stamped with its value.

In Lydia, these coins all weighed exactly the same. A lion's head stamped onto each coin showed it came from Lydia's king, Croesus. Everyone in Lydia accepted them and these coins became the **currency** of Lydia.

⌒ COINS, COINS, AND ⌒ MORE COINS

WORDS2KNOW!

currency: the system of money produced by a government in a country.

dollar: a unit equal to 100 cents in United States money.

Before long, governments of many other countries made their own coins. Some Russian coins were made in the shape of dolphins. Some ancient Chinese coins were shaped like knives and shovels.

One of the easiest shapes to make and carry is a circle. Circular coins came in different sizes and patterns. Some had holes in the middle so they could be carried on a string. Pictures on heavy stamps were pressed into the metals to let everyone know where the coin came from.

Each piece of a Spanish dollar was called a bit. The entire coin was known as *pieces of eight* because it could be cut up into eight pieces.

KNOW YOUR DOUGH

Early Spanish **dollar** coins had lines on them. If a person wanted to buy something that cost less than a dollar, the coin could be cut into smaller pieces along one of the lines. One coin could be cut into eight equal pieces. This saved coin makers from having to make a lot of different coins.

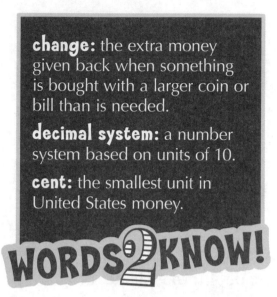

What happened when a coin wasn't cut exactly on the lines? Some people got bigger pieces than others. If coins were going to work as currency, they needed to be the same every time.

Countries began to make coins of different values so people could make **change** easily and fairly. Coin makers added words and numbers to show when coins were made and how much they were worth. Why do you think they added bumpy lines along the edges of coins, called reeded edges? To stop people from scraping gold or silver off the sides of coins.

Two-bits is another name for a quarter. It comes from cutting a Spanish piece of eight into eight pieces. Two pieces of the dollar was the same as one fourth, or a quarter of a dollar.

KNOW YOUR DOUGH

∼ UNITED STATES COINS ∼

The U.S. Mint makes all the coins for the United States. The U.S. Mint made nearly 12 billion coins in 2013! These coins include pennies, nickels, dimes, quarters, half dollars, and dollars.

When the U.S. Mint first started making money in 1792, the government decided to use the **decimal system**. This means all the coins have values that can easily be added up to 100 **cents**. One hundred cents is the same as one dollar.

A decimal looks just like a period, but it is used with numbers instead of words. The number you put to the left of the decimal stands for how many whole dollars you have. The number you put on the right of the decimal is the number of cents you have that are less than one dollar. For example, $1.25 means you have one dollar and 25 cents.

DECIMAL

NUMBER OF WHOLE DOLLARS **$1.25** **CENTS LESS THAN ONE DOLLAR**

DECIMAL MATH

How many ways can you count to 100? Why is it a good plan to use coins that evenly add up to 100 cents? The decimal system makes it easy to count money.

Imagine you're buying a bottle of lemonade that costs $1.25. You give the clerk $2.00. How much change is she going to give you? How many quarters can you expect to get back? How many dimes, nickels, or pennies? The decimal system makes exchanging money a smooth process.

At the U.S. Mint, coins start out as a sheet of metal. The metal is cut into circles, called blanks. The blanks are soaked in special chemicals to make them clean and shiny. Then they're sent through powerful machines that press designs into the front and back at the same time.

The front of each U.S. coin is called the **obverse** or heads side. It has the **image** of a famous person's head. What is on the back of each U.S. coin, which is called the **reverse** or tails side?

15

WORDS2KNOW!

obverse: the front or face of a coin.

image: a picture.

reverse: the back or tail of a coin.

official: when something is named or approved by the government or someone who is in charge.

WORDS 2 KNOW!

~ PENNIES ~

Pennies are copper-colored coins with smooth edges. Their **official** name is the one-cent piece. The sign for cent is ¢. The word *cent* comes from a Latin word that means 100, which is how many cents are in a dollar. You count pennies by ones: one, two, three, four, and so on.

MONEY TALK: PENNIES			
YOU SEE	YOU HAVE	YOU SAY	YOU WRITE
●	1 penny	I have one cent.	1¢ or $0.01
●●●●●●●●●●	10 pennies	I have ten cents.	10¢ or $0.10
(100 pennies shown)	100 pennies	I have one dollar.	$1.00
(125 pennies shown)	125 pennies	I have one dollar and twenty-five cents.	$1.25

What is brown and has a head and a tail, but no legs?
A penny!

When pennies were first made, they had one cent's worth of copper in them. As copper became more expensive, the U.S. Mint made pennies smaller. Then the U.S. Mint started mixing in cheaper metals. Today, pennies are made out of zinc and they have a copper coating.

Look carefully at the fronts and backs of several pennies. What differences can you find? The U.S. Mint makes changes to the design every year. In addition to different dates, you might find different pictures on the fronts and the backs of the pennies.

NICKELS

Nickels are silver-colored coins with smooth edges. The official name of the nickel is the five-cent piece. It is worth the same as five pennies. You count the value of nickels by fives: 5, 10, 15, 20, and so on. One dollar equals 20 nickels.

THE LINCOLN PENNY

Almost all the pennies you'll find have President Abraham Lincoln on the front. Turn the penny over. Pennies made between 1959 and 2008 have the Lincoln Memorial on the back. Look for the statue of Lincoln in the middle of the building. You might need to use a magnifying glass. The penny is the only coin to have a picture of the same person on the front and on the back.

Can you find a penny made later than 2008? What is the design on the reverse side?

KNOW YOUR DOUGH

Before 1866, the nickel was called a half dime and was made of silver. Today, nickels are made of nickel and copper mixed together.

In 1938, there was a contest to design a new nickel to honor former President Thomas Jefferson. On the obverse of this nickel is an image of Jefferson. On the reverse is an image of his home, called Monticello.

In 2004 and 2005, four different designs were made on the reverse of nickels to celebrate the Lewis and Clark expedition. Monticello was returned to the back of the nickel in 2006.

MONEY TALK: NICKELS

YOU SEE	YOU HAVE	YOU SAY	YOU WRITE
	1 nickel	I have five cents.	5¢ or $0.05
	5 nickels	I have twenty-five cents.	25¢ or $0.25
	20 nickels	I have one dollar.	$1.00
	25 nickels	I have one dollar and twenty-five cents.	$1.25

LEWIS AND CLARK

The Lewis and Clark expedition was a journey to explore the land from the Mississippi River west, all the way to the Pacific Coast. It was led by Meriwether Lewis and William Clark. Lewis and Clark left in 1804 and didn't return until 1806. One of their guides and translators, a Native American woman named Sacagawea, is featured on the dollar coin. The Lewis and Clark nickels celebrated the 200-year anniversary of the Lewis and Clark expedition.

DIMES

Dimes are the smallest U.S. coins in size. They have a layer of pure copper through the middle and are coated with a mixture of copper and nickel. They also have reeded edges. The official name for a dime is ten-cent piece. It is worth the same as 10 pennies or two nickels.

Do you recognize the pictures on the front and back of the dime? On the obverse is former President Franklin D. Roosevelt. When he was 39 years old, he caught a disease called polio, which left him unable to walk. As president, he established a research foundation called March of Dimes to encourage people to donate their dimes to help fund polio research.

Why didn't the dime roll down the hill with the nickel?
Because it has twice the common *cents*!

Just for Fun!

MONEY TALK: DIMES

YOU SEE	YOU HAVE	YOU SAY	YOU WRITE
🪙	1 dime	I have ten cents.	10¢ or $0.10
🪙🪙	2 dimes	I have twenty cents.	20¢ or $0.20
🪙🪙🪙🪙🪙 🪙🪙🪙🪙🪙	10 dimes	I have one dollar.	$1.00
🪙🪙🪙🪙 🪙🪙🪙🪙 🪙🪙	12 dimes	I have one dollar and twenty cents.	$1.20

On the reverse side of the dime, the olive branch on the left is for peace. The oak branch on the right is for strength and independence. The torch in the middle stands for liberty. On the side of every dime are 118 reeds.

～ QUARTERS ～

Quarters are silver colored on the outside with a copper layer in the middle. The outer layer is made of copper and nickel mixed together. A quarter is also called a twenty-five-cent piece, but the official name of the quarter is the quarter dollar.

WORDS 2 KNOW!

token: a round piece of metal or plastic that looks like a coin. It is used in place of a coin in some machines.

Have you been to a car wash or ridden on the subway? Many places such as these use metal tokens that look like coins. You use money to buy these tokens. They can be used only at the business that sold them. It is against the law for tokens to be made the same size and of the same materials as U.S. coins.

KNOW YOUR DOUGH

20

Why did the U.S. Mint decide to make quarters instead of 20-cent pieces? Because people already used the word *quarter* to describe two bits of a Spanish pieces of eight. It made sense to stick with a phrase people knew.

MONEY TALK: QUARTERS			
YOU SEE	YOU HAVE	YOU SAY	YOU WRITE
	1 quarter	I have twenty-five cents.	25¢ or $0.25
	2 quarters	I have fifty cents.	50¢ or $0.50
	4 quarters	I have one dollar.	$1.00
	10 quarters	I have two dollars and fifty cents.	$2.50

A picture of former President George Washington has been on the obverse of the quarter since 1932. For many years, an eagle was on the reverse.

In 1999, the U.S. Mint began printing five different variations on the tails side of the quarter each year. The new designs celebrate the individual states, American territories, National Parks, and other important national sites. The U.S. Mint sells special books to collect these different quarters. While you're collecting, can you count the number of ridges on the reeded edges of the quarter? Every quarter has the same number.

HALF DOLLARS

The largest coin used in the United States is the 50-cent piece, officially called the half dollar. It is silver colored with a reeded edge. The outer layers are made of copper and nickel mixed together. Through the middle lies a layer of pure copper, the same as in dimes.

MONEY TALK: HALF DOLLARS

YOU SEE	YOU HAVE	YOU SAY	YOU WRITE
	1 half dollar	I have fifty cents.	50¢ or $0.50
	2 half dollars	I have one dollar.	$1.00
	5 half dollars	I have two dollars and fifty cents.	$2.50

On the obverse of the half dollar is a picture of former President John Kennedy. On the reverse is the Seal of the President of the United States. The seal includes an eagle holding an olive branch to represent peace. The eagle also holds a clutch of arrows, which means that the United States is ready to go to war if it needs to. There are 50 stars, one for each state, in the circle around the seal. What else can you find?

What did the football coach say to the vending machine?
Give me my quarter back!

Just for Fun!

DOLLARS

Dollar coins have been minted in the United States in gold, silver, and other metals. But today, even though they are gold in color, dollar coins have no real gold in them. They are made of layers of metals including copper, zinc, manganese, and nickel mixed together. The same is true of silver dollars. They have no real silver in them.

Dollars are the coins with the greatest value used in the United States. Each dollar is worth 100 pennies or 20 nickels or 10 dimes or 4 quarters or 2 half dollars.

MONEY TALK: DOLLARS			
YOU SEE	YOU HAVE	YOU SAY	YOU WRITE
	1 dollar	I have one dollar.	$1.00
	2 dollars	I have two dollars.	$2.00

Look along the edges of several dollar coins. Are they all the same? How are some different from other coins you know? The edge is the one part of the dollar coin that is going to stay the same for a while. The U.S. Mint is issuing five new dollar designs each year. Four will have a U.S. president on the obverse and the Statue of Liberty on the reverse. The other will have Sacagawea on the obverse and another important Native American on the reverse.

COIN CHART

It's easy to make a coin chart to put in your Money Matters Journal. Use it as you practice counting coins and their values.

SUPPLIES

$ paper

$ pencil

$ ruler

$ coins: penny, nickel, dime, quarter, half-dollar, dollar

$ tape

1 Use the pencil and ruler to draw a grid with seven rows and seven columns.

2 Leave the box in the top left corner empty.

3 Do a rubbing of a penny in the box at the top of the second column and in the far left box of the second row. Write 1¢ in the boxes with the pennies.

	1¢	5¢	10¢	25¢	50¢	100¢
1¢	1					
5¢		1				
10¢			1			
25¢				1		
50¢					1	
100¢						1

HOW TO DO A RUBBING

Put any coin on a flat, sturdy surface. Place a piece of paper over it. Hold a pencil or crayon so you make marks using its flat side, not its tip. Rub over the coin. You will see its image appear on the paper!

4 Do a rubbing of a nickel in the box at the top of the third column and in the far left box of the third row. Write 5¢ in the boxes with the nickels.

5 Do a rubbing of a dime in the box at the top of the fourth column and in the far left box of the fourth row. Write 10¢ in the boxes with the dimes.

6 Do a rubbing of a quarter in the box at the top of the fifth column and in the far left box of the fifth row. Write 25¢ in the boxes with the quarters.

7 Do a rubbing of a half-dollar in the box at the top of the sixth column and in the far left box of the sixth row. Write 50¢ in the boxes with the half dollars.

8 Do a rubbing of a dollar coin in the box at the top of the seventh column and in the far left box of the seventh row. Write 100¢ in the boxes with the dollars.

9 Use what you know about the value of each coin to fill in the chart. How many pennies could you trade for one nickel? How many nickels do you need for one dime? Fill in all the boxes. The toughest box to fill in is how many dimes it takes to equal one quarter! Put your coin chart in the Money Math section of your Money Matters Journal.

25

SUPER SORTING

How well do you know your coins? Here's a fun way to find out.

1 Start by sorting your circles in as many different ways as you can. Sort them by size, color, thickness, design, year, and edges. How many other ways can you sort them?

2 Take out all the metal circles that are not coins. Practice counting your money by putting your coins into piles that equal 100¢ or $1.00. How many different ways can you make 100¢, which is the same as $1.00?

3 On each slip of paper, write down an amount under 50¢. For example, 21¢, 37¢, 49¢. Try to think of numbers that are very different from each other. Put the slips in a pile.

4 Put at least one quarter, two dimes, three nickels, and four pennies in the bag. Draw a slip of paper. Without looking, put your hand in the bag and pull out the coins that make that amount. Is it easy or hard to tell a penny from a nickel or a quarter from a dime?

TRY THIS! Now put all of your coins, tokens, and other metal circles in the bag. Choose a slip of paper with an amount of money on it. How hard is it to pull out the coins that make the right amount?

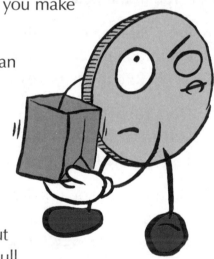

SUPPLIES

$ coins, tokens, and other metal circles such as washers and bottle caps

$ 10 slips of paper

$ pencil

$ paper bag

~ ACTIVITY ~

COIN TESTING

A long time ago, traders tested coins to see if they were made of the right metal. Even today, when you put a coin in a vending machine it gets tested for size, weight, magnetic attraction, and whether or not it conducts electricity. The vending machine wants to know you're using real money! You can do some of the same tests.

SUPPLIES

$ piece of paper
$ pencil
$ coins: penny, nickel, dime, quarter, half dollar, dollar
$ tokens, steel washers, or coins from other countries
$ magnet
$ ruler

1 On the paper, trace a circle around each coin. Label each circle. Use this to test the size of every metal circle you find. If a metal circle does not match a size, it can't be a U.S. coin. If you find a metal circle that does match a coin size, move on to the second test.

2 See if the magnet sticks to the metal circle. If it does, it can't be a U.S. coin. U.S. coins do not have iron in them and are not magnetic. If a magnet doesn't stick, go to the third test.

3 Balance the ruler on one finger. Place the metal circle on one end and the coin that matches its size on the other end. If the stick stays balanced, you have found a good imposter!

What do an old dime (made before 1965) and newer penny (made after 1982) have in common? Even though they are different sizes, they will balance during your third test!

KNOW YOUR DOUGH

27

BILLS

In addition to using metal coins as money, people around the world use thinner, lighter money called **banknotes**, or bills. Why do we need bills when we have coins?

Coins are very useful, but they're heavy to carry around. Another problem with coins is that sometimes countries don't have enough metal to make them. Because of this, hundreds of years ago Chinese rulers encouraged people to exchange their metal coins for pieces of mulberry bark with writing on it. They could use these bark pieces as money.

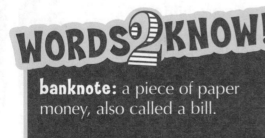

WORDS 2 KNOW!

banknote: a piece of paper money, also called a bill.

28

Just for Fun!

Why was the ranger at the deer park crying?
Because he only had one buck!

In some parts of China, people left their heavy coins with merchants. In exchange, the merchants gave them pieces of leather with the values of the coins written on them. People could trade those leather pieces for goods that added up to those values. Anyone who had a piece of leather could go back to the merchant and trade it back for metal coins. Or, they could use them to buy things.

But too many people made too many different kinds of this money. Eventually, the Chinese government made a law saying only the government could make money. When the Chinese invented a way to make paper from wood, paper money became possible.

If you want to pay in coins for something that costs $100, how heavy will the coins be? Using dollar coins, you'll carry 2 pounds (0.9 kilograms) of coins. Using pennies, you'll have to carry 55 pounds (25 kilograms)!

KNOW YOUR DOUGH

THE BUCK STUCK!

When people from Europe first came to America, they often traded with the Native Americans for deerskins. A buck is a male deer, so sometimes they recorded their trades as being "ten bucks." When traders started using paper money instead of deerskins, the word "buck" stuck!

slang: a different word for something, used mostly in speech.

...THEY USE PAPER MONEY! IT'S GREAT!

Marco Polo was a famous Italian explorer and trader who lived in China during the 1200s. Around 1290 CE, Marco Polo went back to Europe and told everyone about the paper money he had seen in China.

Countries in Europe started running out of metal for coins. So they began using paper for money. Sweden made the first European paper money in 1661.

Greenback is **slang** for U.S. paper money. Banknotes got this name because the first official bills made by the U.S. Treasury had black ink on the front and green ink on the back.

KNOW YOUR DOUGH

AMERICAN MONEY

Before 1861, the U.S. Mint only made coins. Individual states and banks could make their own banknotes, which was very confusing! In 1861, the government made a law that there could be only one type of paper money in America. In 1914, the Federal Reserve opened, and the 12 Federal Reserve Banks became the only places where U.S. banknotes could be printed. All U.S. money is government-backed. This means our money has a value guaranteed by the government.

PS

Watch money being printed, stamped, and cut at a Federal Reserve Bank.

30

BILL BASICS

Money needs to last a long time. It also must be very hard to counterfeit. The U.S. Treasury examined every part of a bill as it worked on new designs for paper money:

* ✳ the size of each bill
* ✳ the paper the bills are printed on
* ✳ the pictures on the bill
* ✳ the ink used to print on a bill
* ✳ the numbers used to identify each bill
* ✳ how much each bill is worth

The first paper money issued in the United States in 1862 came in bills of 5¢, 10¢, 25¢, and 50¢.

KNOW YOUR DOUGH

SIZE

VALUE

PAPER

THE INK

SERIAL NUMBERS

PICTURE

It costs the Treasury between five and 14 cents to make each bill. It all starts with a special paper made by Crane & Company from Massachusetts. Each sheet of paper is printed with 32 bills. After the front and back are printed, the bills are cut so they each measure exactly 2.61 inches (6.6 centimeters) wide and 6.14 inches (15.6 centimeters) long.

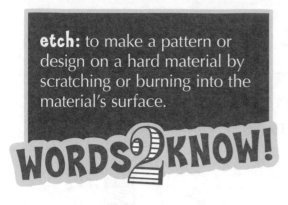

etch: to make a pattern or design on a hard material by scratching or burning into the material's surface.

WORDS2KNOW!

Printing money is different than printing out your homework. For bills, the pictures are **etched** onto metal plates. The plates are covered with ink, the extra ink is wiped off, and then the plate is pressed down onto the paper. Why is money printed this way? Because even the best computer printers can't produce an image with all the details of an etched picture.

WHAT'S ON A BILL?

There are many things to look for on each type of bill. The front has the value of the bill and a picture of a famous person who is no longer alive. Notice the green serial number in two different places. The serial number contains both letters and numbers.

Can you find the seals of the Federal Reserve and the Department of the Treasury? The signatures of the treasurer of the United States and the secretary of the Treasury are underneath these seals.

VALUE PICTURE SERIAL NUMBER

SEALS SIGNATURES

The back of the bill also shows the value of the bill. The value is written in **digits** in the corners and in letters in at least one other place. There is also a picture on the back.

You'll see the official **motto** of the United States here, which is "In God We Trust." Every bill has a tiny number in a clear area on the lower right-hand side. This is the back plate number.

digit: a number.

motto: a sentence or phrase that describes a rule or suggests the use or nature of something.

treaty: an agreement between two or more countries.

VALUE   MOTTO   BACK PLATE NUMBER

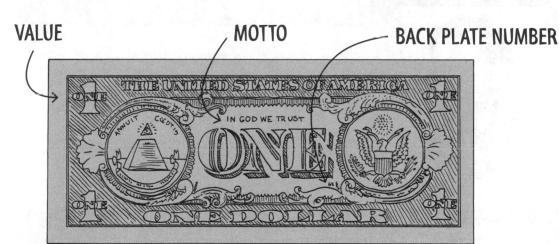

ONE DOLLAR BILL

* **Front:** George Washington, the first president
* **Back:** The Great Seal of the United States
* **Lasts how long?** 5.9 years
* **Tidbit:** The Great Seal is also stamped onto **treaties** and other important papers.

TWO DOLLAR BILL

* **Front:** Thomas Jefferson, the second president
* **Back:** The signing of the Declaration of Independence
* **Lasts how long?** There are so few, no one keeps track.
* **Tidbit:** So few people use $2 bills that some people think they are fake!

FIVE DOLLAR BILL

* **Front:** Abraham Lincoln, the 16th president
* **Back:** The Lincoln Memorial
* **Lasts how long?** 4.9 years
* **Tidbit:** The picture on the back of the $5 bill is the same one pictured on the back of the penny.

TEN DOLLAR BILL

* **Front:** Alexander Hamilton, the first secretary of the Treasury
* **Back:** The U.S. Treasury Building
* **Lasts how long?** 4.2 years
* **Tidbit:** Hamilton's picture faces left. All the other pictures on the fronts of U.S. bills face right.

TWENTY DOLLAR BILL

* **Front:** Andrew Jackson, the seventh president
* **Back:** The White House
* **Lasts how long?** 7.7 years
* **Tidbit:** When he was president, Andrew Jackson fought against the creation of the Bank of the United States.

FIFTY DOLLAR BILL

* **Front:** Ulysses S. Grant, the 18th president
* **Back:** The U.S. Capitol
* **Lasts how long?** 3.7 years
* **Tidbit:** In 1969, for the first time, the words around the Treasury Seal were printed in English instead of in Latin.

ONE HUNDRED DOLLAR BILL

* **Front:** Benjamin Franklin, inventor and **Founding Father**
* **Back:** Independence Hall, Philadelphia, Pennsylvania
* **Lasts how long?** 15 years
* **Tidbit:** This is the only bill to have a picture of a building that is not in Washington, D.C.

WORDS 2 KNOW!

Founding Father: an important person in the founding of the United States.

CODED CASH

If you look at the bottom of the pyramid on the back of a $1 bill, you will see the letters MDCCLXXVI. These letters are Roman numerals! What number do they represent? It's like a code. Use the chart here to figure it out.

How do you use Roman numerals? If you see an I before a letter, it means to subtract one. So the number four is written as IV (five minus one). Nine is written as IX (10 minus one). This book was first printed in 2014. If you want to write it in Roman numerals, you would write MM (2,000) X (10) IV (five minus one), so MMXIV.

ROMAN NUMERAL	VALUE
I	1
V	5
X	10
L	50
C	100
D	500
M	1,000

What number is written on the bill? Why is that number important? Can you write the year of your birth in Roman numerals? Where else do you see Roman numerals?

Before 1949, all the treasurers of the United States were men. Since 1949, all the treasurers of the United States have been women. A treasurer is the person who is in charge of the money.

KNOW YOUR DOUGH

MONEY TALK

The phrases on money in the United States are written in Latin.

* *E Pluribus Unum:* Out of many, one

* *Annuit Coeptis:* S/he has favored our undertakings

* *Novus Ordo Seclorum:* New order of the ages

PAPER MONEY

SUPPLIES

$ scissors
$ copy paper
$ waxed paper
$ construction paper
$ tissue paper
$ wrapping paper
$ cotton fabric
$ polyester fabric
$ Money Matters Journal
$ ruler
$ pens
$ pencils
$ dollar bill
$ markers
$ bowl of water
$ liquid soap
$ towel

Some people call bills paper money, but that isn't exactly right. Most paper is made out of wood. U.S. bills are made out of cotton and linen, which are two types of plants. The bills you save and spend are more like your clothes than the paper you write on! Why? Because the cotton and linen make the bills last longer. Bills need to fold easily but be hard to tear. They need to be easy to print on, and hold on to the ink so it doesn't wash off or fade.

Think about how many different times a bill might go in and out of a pocket, wallet, or cash register. What material would make a banknote that will last?

1 Cut a rectangle out of each type of paper or cloth. Each rectangle should be 3 inches by 6 inches (7½ centimeters by 15 centimeters).

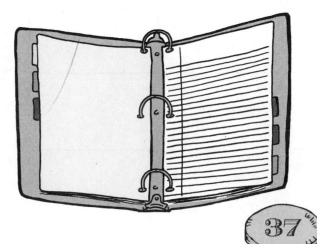

2 Make a test chart in your Money Matters Journal like the one on the next page. Keep it in the Money Facts section. You will use one row for each material you test.

PROJECT CONTINUED ON NEXT PAGE.

MATERIALS TEST CHART

MATERIAL	FOLDING TEST	WRITING TEST	WASHING TEST
dollar bill	very sturdy	easy to write on	does not fade or fall apart
copy paper			
waxed paper			
construction paper			
tissue paper			
wrapping paper			
cotton fabric			
polyester fabric			

FUNNY MONEY

Other colors have been added to special areas on the bills throughout the years. Today, you can see yellow, red, blue, and gold in some bills. Some of the inks will even change color when you move them in the light! These inks were added to make it harder for people to make counterfeit money. Holograms have also been added to bills. These special pictures are produced by a laser and look three-dimensional.

3 Feel the real dollar bill. Feel the other materials. Fold each piece in half and open it back up at least 100 times each. Are any starting to tear? Write down your observations in your chart.

4 Now make a mark on each rectangle using the pencil, pen, and marker. Try to rub each mark off using just your finger. Record your observations on your chart.

5 Add a few drops of liquid soap to the bowl of water. Put the dollar bill in the water and swish it around. Rub it between your fingers. Swish it some more. Take it out of the water and place it on the towel to dry. Do the same thing with your other rectangle samples. Record your observations in your chart.

6 If you had to make your own bills, which material would you choose? Why? Make a few extra rectangles of that material and use it to make your own money later in this chapter!

You would have to fold a new dollar bill back and forth more than 4,000 times before it would tear!

KNOW YOUR DOUGH

DOLLAR DETECTIVE

You can see how much the designs of paper money have changed by comparing $1 and $5 bills.

The $1 bill is the simplest and hasn't changed much since 1963. Most people don't bother making fake ones because it is too much work for too little money! The $5 bill was redesigned in 2007 with features to make it hard to copy.

SUPPLIES

$ Money Matters Journal

$ U.S. $1 bill and $5 bill

$ magnifying lens

$ bright light

1 Use a sheet of paper from your Money Matters Journal and create a chart. This is where you can keep track of your observations. Headings can include: ink, watermarks, plastic thread, other special features.

2 Count how many different colors of ink you see on each bill. Which one uses more colors?

3 One bill has two hidden items, called watermarks, plus a wide plastic thread. You can only see these when you hold a bill up to a light. Hold up each bill so a bright light shines through it. What are the hidden watermarks? Where is the plastic thread?

4 One bill honors the 13 colonies by having pictures that include 13 items. Which bill is it? How many different sets of 13 can you find?

BIG BANKNOTES

Up until 1969, the Federal Reserve made banknotes worth $500, $1,000, $5,000, $10,000, and even $100,000! You would need only 10 of the biggest notes to be carrying around 1 million dollars. The biggest banknote you can get now is $100.

5 One bill has microprinting. These are tiny letters that are hard to see. Use a magnifying lens to look around the edges on the front of each bill. Can you find the tiny words that are repeated over and over? What other things do you notice about each bill?

When Russia was in charge of the area we call Alaska, it used sealskin to make its bills! Today, some countries make their bills out of plastic.

KNOW YOUR DOUGH

6 Use these ideas to start designing your own bill. Think about how much it should be worth. Should there be a picture on it? Do you want the picture to be a person, animal, plant, building, or something else? Why? Keep your chart and the designs for your bill in your Money Matters Journal in the Money Facts section.

TRY THIS! Take a close look at the other U.S. bills. Can you find special features on each one? Add your observations of each bill to your chart.

TRY THIS, TOO! A stack of any 233 U.S. bills is 1 inch (2½ centimeters) tall. How many U.S. bills does it take to reach your height? Use the formula below to figure out the answer:

your height in inches x 233 = number of bills

COUNTING CHALLENGE

You can use real banknotes in this counting activity if you have them. But if you don't have them, make your own for the counting challenge!

1 Decorate the index cards using a different marker for each type of bill. Create the obverse side only for each of the following bills:

- $1 bills—10 cards

- $5 bills—six cards

- $10 bills—five cards

- $20 bills—three cards

- $50 bills—two cards

- $100 bills—one card

2 Start a new page in the Counting Money section of your Money Matters Journal.

3 Count the value of each different type of card and record it on a separate line.

- For example, you have 10 of the $1 cards. That's $1 x 10 or:

$$1 + 1 + 1 + 1 + 1 + 1 + 1 + 1 + 1 + 1 = \$10$$

4 Add a separate line of value for each bill so that there are six different lines of value total.

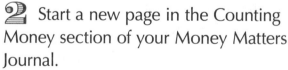

5 Mix all the cards in a pile, face down. Pick two cards. Write down the cards and how much the total value is.

- For example, if you pick $5 and $100, write:

  $5 + $100 = $105.

- If you pick $10 and $10, write down:

  $10 + $10 = $20.

6 Keep picking two cards at a time and writing down their values until only one card remains.

7 Mix all the cards again. This time, pick three cards at a time. Write down the cards and how much the total value is. Keep picking three cards at a time and writing down their values until no more cards are left.

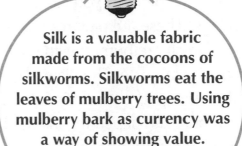

Silk is a valuable fabric made from the cocoons of silkworms. Silkworms eat the leaves of mulberry trees. Using mulberry bark as currency was a way of showing value.

KNOW YOUR DOUGH

8 Keep adding more cards to the number you pick until you count all of them at the same time. Most of the time when you pick the groups of cards, you will have some left over at the end. What you are doing is dividing the cards. When they don't divide evenly, the ones left over are called the remainder. Which groupings had remainder cards?

TRY THIS! Using the same cards, figure out three ways to make $15. Keep the cards in a Ziploc bag in your Money Matters Journal for later.

ETCH YOUR SKETCH

Most of the pictures you can see on U.S. bills are etchings. These are pictures made of thousands of lines, which are burned with chemicals and light onto a metal plate. The plate is covered in ink, and then wiped clean. When the plate is pressed down onto the paper, the ink left between the lines is transferred onto the paper. You can make your own etched line drawing.

Use the paper to learn how the process works. Then you can try etching your own design on the rectangles you chose during the material test.

1 Cover your table or desk with newspaper.

2 Using wax crayons, draw your design, completely coloring the paper. To make it look like a real bill, plan where you want to see different colors.

3 When the paper is completely covered with crayon color, paint over the entire paper with black paint.

4 Let the paint dry. If you can still see the color underneath, paint another coat of black on and let it dry.

5 Use the tip of the toothpick to draw your bill design. You will be scraping off the black paint to show the colors below. Don't press too hard or you'll poke a hole through the paper!

BANKS

What do you think of when you hear the word *bank*? A small toy pig with a slot in the top? A big building with heavy doors and guards? Both of these are banks! A bank is a place where money is kept.

Once coins were invented, people had something new to worry about. Coins are small and easy to lose—or easily stolen. Where could people keep their coins safe? Where do you keep your coins?

Long ago, people put their coins in jars and pots. They hid the jars under their beds. But what if the house burned down? Some people even buried their coins underground. Digging up your money before shopping is dirty work!

45

WORDS2KNOW!

temple: a building used as a place of religion.

account: a record of the money put in or taken out of a bank.

deposit: when money is added to a bank account.

withdrawal: when money is taken out of a bank account.

transaction: a deposit to an account or a withdrawal from an account.

Merchants began to take care of people's coins. In some countries, people could leave their coins at a **temple**. People had to trust the merchants and temple workers to keep track of who gave them coins and how many they gave. The information was often recorded on clay tablets.

THE BIRTH OF BANKS

As money became more and more popular, some people saw the chance to start a new business. Banking! Bankers make money by taking care of other people's money.

Anyone with money can open an **account** at a bank. Money put into a bank account is called a **deposit**. Money taken out of a bank account is called a **withdrawal**. Each deposit or withdrawal is called a **transaction**.

Imagine you are the banker. Your first customer deposits $10 into his or her account. The second one deposits $15. The third one withdraws $5. The fourth one withdraws $2. What color are the banker's eyes?

Remember—*YOU* are the banker!

Just for Fun!

Every account is given a unique identification number. Bankers use the identification number every time there is a transaction in an account. Why do you think a number works better than using names? Have you ever met someone with the same name as you?

CREDIT CARDS

Some adults use credit cards to buy expensive things such as vacations or new appliances. A credit card is a plastic card with an account number on it that is connected to a bank account. Credit cards allow you to buy something without paying money right away. Instead, you agree to pay a little money every month until you have paid the whole balance.

Credit cards are convenient, but they can be hard to manage. Some people keep charging money until they owe the bank thousands of dollars they don't have. If you ever have a credit card as an adult, be sure to be very careful with how you use it!

You can track a $1 bill! Ask an adult for permission to go on the Internet. Go to the website wheresgeorge.com and follow the instructions to see where your "George" has been!

KNOW YOUR DOUGH

How do banks **earn** money? They charge **fees**. A bank might charge a fee of $3 each month for every account. Or it could charge a fee of 5 cents for every transaction. Banks can even charge fees if you make too many transactions in a month or don't keep enough money in your account.

47

WORDS 2 KNOW!

earn: to get something in return for doing work.

fee: a charge for a service.

interest: the fee charged or paid for the use of money.

loan: an amount of money that is borrowed and has to be paid back.

WORDS 2 KNOW!

Banks also earn money by charging **interest**. When people buy a house or a car, they often go to a bank for a **loan**. This is when someone borrows money from the bank. He or she promises to pay some of it back each month until he or she has paid all of the money back. The bank charges a fee for loaning this money, and this fee is called interest.

What do banks do with the money they earn from fees and interest? Banks use that extra money to pay their workers and pay their bills. They also use it to pay interest. When you keep money in a savings account at a bank, the bank pays you a very small amount of money each month. Why do you think banks charge more interest on loans than they pay on accounts?

CURRENCY EXCHANGE

Banks have other jobs as well. There are more than 225 different currencies from different countries in the world. In the United States, when people have a different currency, they can't use it to buy things in stores. They have to go to a bank and exchange it for U.S. currency. And the bank charges a fee to make this exchange!

PS Use this interactive chart to find the rates of currency exchange. How much is one American dollar worth in Canada? In Britain?

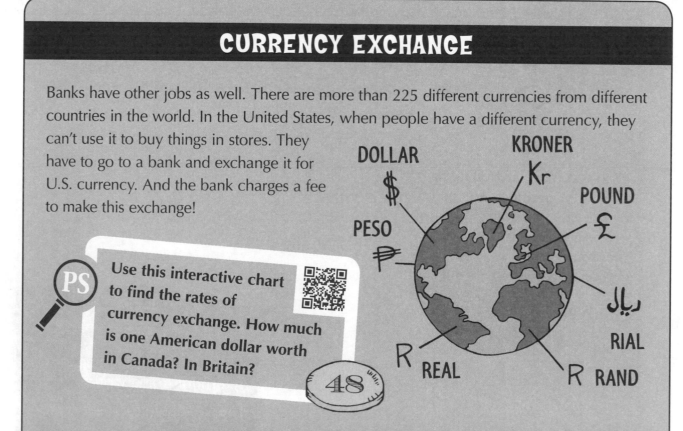

DOLLAR
$

PESO
₱

KRONER
Kr

POUND
£

ریال
RIAL

R RAND

R REAL

48

MANAGING YOUR ACCOUNT

When banks first started, you had to be at the bank to make a deposit or a withdrawal. To make it easier for account holders to use their money, checks were invented. Checks are slips of paper that act like money messengers.

Each check has your name, address, account number, and the bank information printed on it. When a person who owns an account writes a check, it tells his or her bank to give the person holding the check a certain amount of money.

After computers were invented, people could send those money messages without writing anything down on paper. Now many people just send messages over the Internet telling their banks who to send money to.

All day, every day, money is being moved from one bank to another. There are millions and millions and millions of transactions. It's a good thing that banks have computers to keep track of whose money is going where.

Even if different countries call their money dollars and cents, that doesn't mean it's worth the same amount! Dollars in the United States have a different value than dollars in Canada. The **exchange rate** of U.S. dollars for Canadian dollars is around 92¢ for one Canadian dollar. This rate can change over time.

KNOW YOUR DOUGH

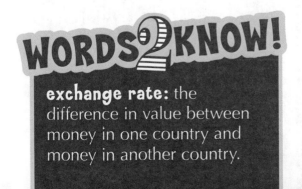

WORDS 2 KNOW!

exchange rate: the difference in value between money in one country and money in another country.

UNDERSTANDING PLACE VALUE

Banks handle money—a LOT of money! When people make deposits and withdrawals, they have to be able to count their coins and bills and write down the values. Since you will likely open a bank account some day, now is a good time to learn those skills!

1 Write each digit, 0 through 9, on separate cards. Make four of each card. If you are using playing cards, take out all the face cards. Change the aces to the number 1 and make the 10s into zeros.

2 Mix up the cards and spread them out face down so you can't see the numbers. Pick three cards and turn them over.

3 In the Money Math section of your Money Matters Journal, write down the three numbers using the decimal system. Remember what you learned from chapter one. Two numbers go on the right side of the decimal for cents. One number goes on the left side of the decimal for dollars.

1 NUMBER HERE (DOLLARS)   **$1.25**   2 NUMBERS HERE (CENTS)

DECIMAL

4 How many different ways can you write three numbers you picked using this system? If your cards were a 3, 5, and 7, you could write $3.57. This means you have three dollars and fifty-seven cents.

5 With these three numbers you could also write $3.75 and $5.73 and $5.37 and $7.35 and $7.53. Say out loud how much money each number represents.

6 Circle the number that has the biggest value. Put a square around the number that has the smallest value.

7 Put those cards to the side. Continue picking three new cards and writing down and saying all the possible combinations.

TRY THIS! What happens when you draw four cards at a time? How many numbers go on the left of the decimal point now? Save your cards for the next activity.

Sometimes people use the slang word *Benjamins* when they talk about $100 bills. Can you figure out why? Take a look at a $100 bill and the picture that is on the front of the banknote.

KNOW YOUR DOUGH

BORROWING MONEY

Who borrows money from a bank? Your parents might need to borrow money to buy a new family car. The bank will loan them the money they need. Your parents will sign loan papers that say they promise to pay back a little bit of the money, plus additional interest, each month. It can take between four and six years to pay for a car this way.

TRADING UP

You can play this game alone or with friends. The goal of the game is to create the hand with the highest value.

1 Cut out one small round dot to use as a decimal point for each player.

2 Mix up the 40 cards labeled 1 through 9. Deal each player four cards. Without looking at his or her cards, each player lays them face down in a row. The decimal point goes in the middle with two cards on the left and two on the right.

3 Put the rest of the cards in a pile, face down. Turn over the top card and place it to the side of the pile.

4 The first player turns over any one card. Then the player picks a new card—either the card facing up next to the pile or the card on top of the pile. If the player wants, he or she can replace the face up card with the picked-up card. Then either the card picked up or the one replaced must be discarded into the face-up pile.

5 Each player takes a turn until all the cards in the pile have been turned over. The player with the largest amount of money wins!

TRY THIS! If you play this game several times, you can keep score using the Bank Book activity on page 54!

MAKE A BANK

The most basic bank is a place where you put your money to keep it safe. You can make a bank out of almost anything—a jar, bottle, or even an old sock.

HINT: A plastic bottle with a narrow neck will make it harder to get your big coins and folded bills out. If you can't get them out, you can't spend them! This might be a good thing.

SUPPLIES

$ clean, dry plastic bottle with a wide mouth, such as an old detergent bottle

$ scissors

$ paper torn into small pieces

$ 1 cup flour

$ 1 cup warm water

$ bowl and spoon

$ paint and paint brush

1 Ask an adult to cut a long ¼-inch-wide (½-centimeter-wide) slit in one side of the bottle. This slit should be near the top of the bottle.

2 Mix the flour and water in the bowl until it's smooth. Dip each paper piece into the mixture and squeeze the extra off between two fingers. Smooth each piece over the surface of the bottle.

3 Keep adding overlapping pieces until the entire bottle is covered. Let it dry overnight.

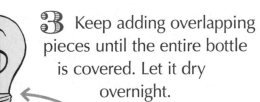

Some people say you should "sock your money away." Does that give you a clue where people used to hide their money?

KNOW YOUR DOUGH

4 Decorate your bank with paint. You can make it look like an animal sitting up, a plant, a statue, or anything you can imagine. When the paint is dry, start filling your bank with your coins and bills.

53

BANK REGISTER

How do you know how much money you have in the bank? The bank keeps track of your money, but you should too. That way you always know how much money you have in the bank. When you open an account the bank gives you a bank register. Each time you make a deposit to or a withdrawal from your account, record the amount in your bank register. It's a very good habit!

1 Start a new page in the My Savings section in your Money Matters Journal. Use the ruler to draw five columns on the page. Label the columns like this:

DATE	TRANSACTION	DEPOSIT (+)	WITHDRAWAL (-)	BALANCE

2 Imagine you are opening a bank account on January 5 with a deposit of $25. On the first line in column one, write January 5. Write "Opening account" in column two. Write "$25.00" in column three. Leave column four empty because you are not withdrawing money. Write "$25.00" in column five.

DATE	TRANSACTION	DEPOSIT (+)	WITHDRAWAL (-)	BALANCE
January 5	Opening account	$25.00		$25.00

3 Imagine your crazy aunt celebrates Groundhog's Day by sending you $15. You decide to deposit all $15 of that money into your bank account. You record this on line 2. Under column one, write "February 2." Write "Groundhog's gifts" in column two. Write "$15.00" in column 3. Do not write anything in column 4 since you are not withdrawing money. Since you are adding more money, look up to the previous balance in line one. Then add $25 (your previous balance) + $15 (your deposit) = $40. Write "$40.00" in column five. This is your new balance.

DATE	TRANSACTION	DEPOSIT (+)	WITHDRAWAL (-)	BALANCE
January 5	Opening account	$25.00		$25.00
February 2	Groundhog's gifts	$15.00		$40.00

4 On February 11, you go to the bank to withdraw $8 to buy Valentine's cards. Put the entry into your bank register like this:

DATE	TRANSACTION	DEPOSIT (+)	WITHDRAWAL (-)	BALANCE
January 5	Opening account	$25.00		$25.00
February 2	Groundhog's gifts	$15.00		$40.00
February 11	Money for cards		$8.00	$32.00

5 Why is there a "32.00" in column five? You had a previous balance of $40 (from line two). You withdrew $8. $40 − $8 = $32.

6 To make more deposits and withdrawals, use the results from your Trading Up game on page 52. Everyone starts with a balance of $25.00. The person with a winning hand gets to record his or her number as a deposit. Everyone else records their numbers as withdrawals.

BIG NUMBERS

SUPPLIES

$ Money Matters
  Journal

$ pencil

Sometimes numbers get very big when we talk about money! For example, in 2013 there were 11,906,940,000 coins minted for use in the United States. That number is really big. What does it mean? How do you say it?

1 Notice how the digits are put in groups of three, starting from the right. Each group of three digits has a comma between them. In the Money Math section of your journal, practice writing a long number. Put commas in between the groups of three, starting from the right.

NUMBERS IN GROUPS OF THREE

11,906,940,000

GROUPS SEPARATED
BY COMMAS

Each place in these groups of three has a name. In order, from left to right, the place names are hundreds, tens, ones. These place names are the same in every group of three.

11,906,940,000

HUNDREDS

TENS

ONES

This can be really easy to think about with money.

- If you have one $100 bill, one $10 bill, and one $1 bill, you write it as $111.

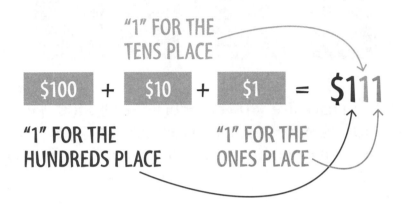

"1" FOR THE TENS PLACE

$100 + $10 + $1 = **$111**

"1" FOR THE HUNDREDS PLACE

"1" FOR THE ONES PLACE

- If you have three $100 bills ($100, $100, $100), four $10 bills ($10, $10, $10, $10), and nine $1 bills ($1, $1, $1, $1, $1, $1, $1, $1, $1), you write it as $349.

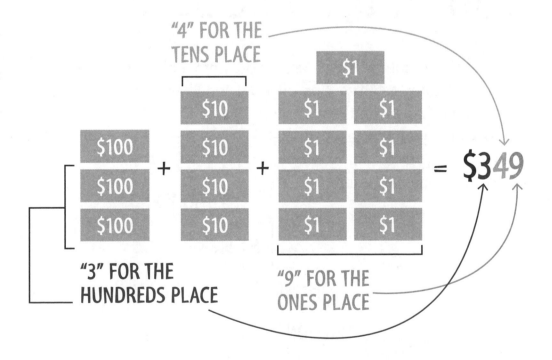

"4" FOR THE TENS PLACE

$100 + $10 + $1 = **$349**

"3" FOR THE HUNDREDS PLACE

"9" FOR THE ONES PLACE

57

PROJECT CONTINUED ON NEXT PAGE.

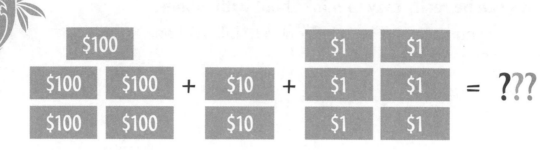

2 What if you have five $100 dollar bills ($100, $100, $100, $100, $100), two $10 bills ($10, $10), and six $1 bills ($1, $1, $1, $1, $1, $1)? Practice changing the numbers and writing them down in your Money Matters Journal.

Each group of three has a group name.

TRILLION   BILLION   MILLION   THOUSAND   HUNDRED

100,000,000,000,000

3 Copy the big numbers staircase below onto a clean sheet of paper in the Money Math section of your Money Matters Journal. By filling in the steps with the matching groups of three, you will easily be able to read your big number simply by climbing the stairs!

HUNDRED

THOUSAND

MILLION

BILLION

TRILLION

4 Start with the group of three numbers on the right side of your big number on the top of the staircase. This is the hundreds group. Go left down the stairs as you copy the next group of three numbers on the top of each line.

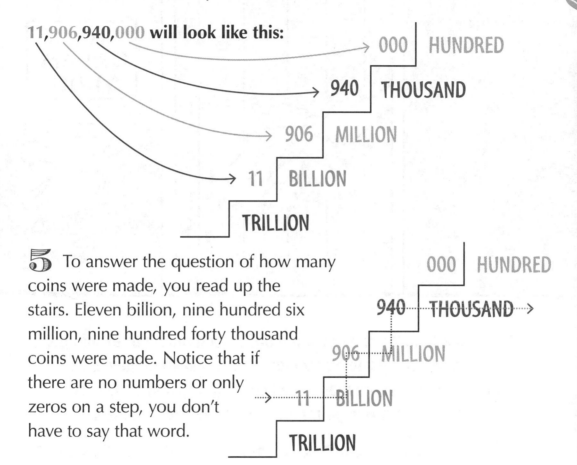

11,906,940,000 will look like this:

000 | HUNDRED
940 | THOUSAND
906 | MILLION
11 | BILLION
TRILLION

5 To answer the question of how many coins were made, you read up the stairs. Eleven billion, nine hundred six million, nine hundred forty thousand coins were made. Notice that if there are no numbers or only zeros on a step, you don't have to say that word.

000 | HUNDRED
940 | THOUSAND →
906 | MILLION
11 | BILLION
TRILLION

6 Here's one for you to try. In 2013, JP Morgan Chase and Company was the bank in the United States with the most money in deposits. How much did it have? $1,128,510,000,000. Draw a new set of stair steps in your Money Matters Journal. Start by putting the group of three zeros on the right side on the top step. Fill in the other steps going down. Then read it up to say that number!

USING MONEY

Money is a tool. What work can it do? As a medium of exchange, you can use money to buy things. You can save money to use later. You can share money by donating it to someone else. Or you can invest your money to make more money.

How do you get money? Kids are often given money for a special celebration, such as a birthday. Some parents give their children money each week as an **allowance**. Kids can earn money by working around their house, helping their neighbors, or selling lemonade. Can you think of ways to earn money?

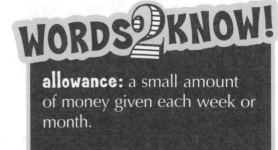

allowance: a small amount of money given each week or month.

It's a good idea to plan what to do with your money before you even get it. Is there a new book you want to buy? If you don't have enough money to buy it, you can save up until you do. Would you like to donate money to a project that needs it? Do you want to open a bank account and earn interest? There are lots of ways to handle your money well.

A family in New York City picks up all the coins they find lying on sidewalks, streets, or floors. In just one year, they found $1,013!

KNOW YOUR DOUGH

A budget is a plan. It helps you decide what you want to do with your money. And it helps you reach those goals. The main choices in a budget are to spend, save, share, and invest. The first step in making a budget is to think about your four choices.

SPENDING MONEY

Spending money is simple. If you have enough money, you can buy what you want! But have you ever spent money and later wished you hadn't? Sometimes people **regret** spending their money on things they don't need. Try to be smart about the things you buy. Ask yourself if you will still be happy with your purchase next week or next month. If you aren't sure, hold onto your money!

WORDS 2 KNOW!

regret: to feel sad or sorry about something you did.

NEEDS OR WANTS?

There are two big groups of things to buy. One group is things that you need. A need is something you must have in order to stay alive and healthy and be able to learn and grow. You need shelter, food, water, clothes, and school supplies.

A want is something you would like to have, but that you can live without. This includes things such as toys, candy, and movies. It can include some clothes that you want but don't need. Most of the time, your parents or other adults will pay for the things you need. They may expect you to use your own money to buy the things you want.

Look at the choices in the chart. You have $30 to spend. Circle one thing in each row. Add up the costs. Do you have enough money to buy your first choice of everything? How can you balance your wants and needs?

NEED	OPTION A	OPTION B
Breakfast	Pancakes, $2	Cereal, $1
Winter Coat	Purple, $18	Green, $12
Drink	Juice, $2	Water, Free
Shoes	Basketball, $15	Regular, $10
Notebook	Fancy, $2	Plain, $1

If you circled each item in the first column, you would need:
$2 + $18 + $2 + $15 + $2 = $39.

If you circled each item in the second column, you would need:
$1 + $12 + $10 + 1 = $24.

You don't have enough money to buy everything in the first column. How many different combinations of items can you pick and stay under $30? Do the math in the Money Math section of your Money Matters Journal.

SMART KIDS' MONEY TIP #1

Take only a little bit of your spending money with you when you go to a store. If you find something you really want, you can go back later to get it. This gives you time to think about it—and maybe you'll decide you don't really want it.

SAVING MONEY

Saving is the opposite of spending. It means putting your money in a safe place, such as your bank at home. It's a good idea to save a portion of any money you receive.

Even if you aren't saving to buy something special, saving money now is good training for saving money when you're older. As an adult you'll need to save a lot of money when you want to buy a house or a car.

SMART KIDS' MONEY TIP #2

Tape the price and a picture of an item you really want to purchase onto your piggy bank. Then, every time you are tempted to spend your money on something else, you will be reminded of your real goal.

What kind of horse is on the Kentucky state quarter?
It's a quarter horse!

Just for Fun!

SHARING MONEY

Sharing money is something you can do to help make the world a better place. People around the world need help buying food, clothes, and shelter. Many children need money to pay for school. Some people need money for medicine, clean water, to take care of animals, clean up trash, or rebuild houses that were wrecked by storms.

There are many ways to share money. You can put your change in special donation jars at stores. You can give money at church or during fundraisers. If everyone who has money shares just a little bit, everyones' lives can improve!

SMART KIDS' MONEY TIP #3

Find something that you care about and share money with projects that are important to you. New books for the library, equipment for a kids' sports team, or providing shelter for people who don't have homes are a few ideas.

INVESTING MONEY

Investing means putting your money to work to make more money. A good rule is to invest only money that you won't need for a long time, maybe even years! Once you invest your money, you need to be patient and let it grow.

How can money make money? When you deposit your money in a bank, the bank uses your money to make loans to other people. Those people pay a fee, called interest, to borrow the bank's money. Part of that interest is used to pay you for letting the bank use your money.

Banks pay more to people who promise to invest their money for longer, such as two years, five years, or even 10 years. These types of long-term savings accounts are called certificate of deposit accounts, or CDs for short.

Your Bank
Invest in a 5 year high-interest CD today!

Savings Account	5 Year CD
0.25% interest rate	1.5% interest rate

Sign up today and receive a free gift while supplies last! Click here to visit our website for more details!

Where do penguins keep their money?
In a snow bank!

Just for Fun!

SMART KIDS' MONEY TIP #4

Ask a bank how much money you need to open an account. Usually it's $25. When you have saved that much, ask your parents to help you open the account. Keep track of how your money grows every year. Later, you can ask for help investing in a CD at a bank or investing in companies on the **stock market**.

WORDS2KNOW!

stock market: a real and virtual place where people buy and sell their investment loans in different companies.

65

POCKETS PLAN

Keep money in your pockets with this fun budget plan.

SUPPLIES
$ 4 sheets of paper
$ pencil
$ ruler
$ Money Matters Journal
$ calculator

1 Make a fold about 1 inch (2½ centimeters) wide along the short side of one sheet of paper. Crease it.

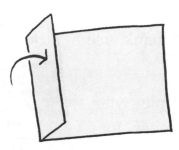

2 Turn the paper over. Make a fold along one long side of the sheet about one-third of the way from the long edge. Crease it. There should be a small flap on top from your first fold.

3 Fold the long unfolded side over the middle so that it covers your first long fold. Tuck the top edge under the flap. Crease the fold.

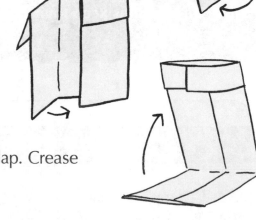

4 Fold up the bottom so that the bottom edge meets the top edge. Tuck the bottom edge under the top flap. Crease the fold. This is one pocket.

5 Make three more paper pockets. Label one pocket "Save," one pocket "Spend," one pocket "Share," and one pocket "Invest."

SAVE   SPEND   SHARE

6 Write your money goals down on the matching pocket. Include exactly how much money you need for each goal.

7 Make a My Budget page in the My Money section of your journal. Draw a table like this on the My Budget page. Use your own numbers!

INVEST

DATE	JUNE 1	JUNE 8	JUNE 9	JUNE 15
INCOME	$5, allowance	$5, allowance	$25, birthday	$5, allowance
SPEND	$1	$1	$10	
SAVE Book, $5 Bike basket, $12	$1 $1	$1 $1	$3 $5	
SHARE Adopt a zoo animal, $15	$1	$1	$2	
INVEST Open a savings account, $25	$1	$1	$5	

8 The rows list how you split your **income** into each goal. If you add the numbers in each column, it should equal your income at the top.

9 Every time you get money, look at your budget. Put the planned amount in each pocket. You will know you have reached a goal when you have the right amount of money in a pocket!

The expression "deep pockets" means to have a lot of money!

KNOW YOUR DOUGH

WORDS 2 KNOW!

income: money that comes in from work, an allowance, or an investment.

DOUBLE DELIGHT

To see how just a little bit can add up, try this amazing demonstration!

1 Pretend you decide to donate one grain of rice each day of the month to a hungry person. Put one grain on each day of the month and record the number of grains on Day One in the Money Math section of your journal. Tell a friend what you are doing.

YOUR RICE

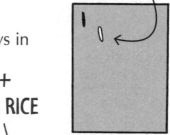

2 On the second day of the month, your friend decides to do the same thing for the rest of the days in the month. Add one more grain to Day Two and each day of the month after that. In your Money Matters Journal, record the number of grains on Day Two of your calendar. Each of you tell one more friend what you are doing.

YOUR RICE + YOUR FRIEND'S RICE

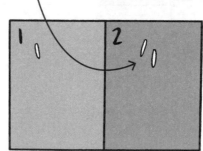

3 On the third day of the month, the two other friends decide they are going to give one grain of rice each day for the rest of the month. Add two more grains on Day Three and every following day. Record the number of grains on Day Three of your calendar in your journal. Each of you tell one more friend what you are doing.

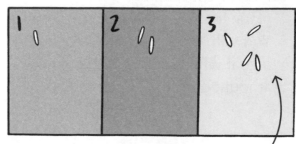

YOUR RICE + YOUR FRIEND'S RICE + YOUR 2 NEW FRIENDS' RICE

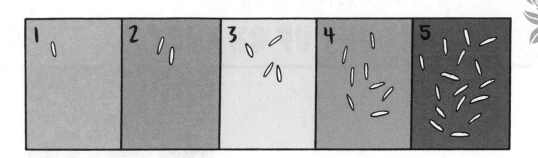

4 Continue this same pattern for each day of the month. On Day Four, there will be eight grains of rice, and eight friends will ask one more person to add a grain of rice each day. On Day Five, there will be 16 grains of rice and 16 people will ask a friend to join them. How long can you keep going before you run out of rice?

5 The rice on your calendar shows the power of doubling. If you kept on doubling the amount of rice each day, how many grains of rice would there be on Day 30? You might want to use your calculator to figure it out! Can you read this very large number?

THINK ABOUT IT:

If you traded each grain of rice for a penny, how much money would have been donated? In our imaginary story, you contributed the most—30¢, which is one penny every day.

Many companies get loans from people instead of banks. When people loan a company money, they are investing in that company. It can be **risky**, because the company may not be able to pay people back. But if the company does well, it will pay much more interest than a bank! There are many ways to invest in a company, but a common way is to buy stocks on the stock market.

KNOW YOUR DOUGH

WORDS2KNOW!

risky: an investment that might lose value.

COUNT UP CHANGE

When you follow a budget, you divide your money into parts. You can do that by using the skills you learned in sorting. To figure out how much money you have left to save, practice counting up change.

1 Sort your money so there is a different value in each container. Coins should go in the round tubs, bills in the boxes.

2 Set up your money like a cash register. Put the tubs of coins in front of you in order, from the largest (25¢) on the left to the smallest (1¢) on the right. Place the bills in the boxes behind the coins.

3 Look at the numbers in the Pockets Plan activity chart. On June 1, you have $1 saved toward a $5 book. How much more do you need to save?

SUPPLIES

$ 4 small round plastic tubs, such as clean food containers

$ 2 boxes about the size and shape of a dollar bill

$ real or play money, including 4 pennies, 2 nickels, 2 dimes, 3 quarters, five $1 bills and two $5 bills

$ pencil

$ 6 slips of paper

$ Money Matters Journal

$ old receipts or store ads (optional)

- Pull out a $1 bill. Put it to your left as you say "1."

- Then start at 2 and count as you pull out dollar bills one at a time and put them on your right. **So you will say "2, 3, 4, 5."**

$1		$1	$1	$1	$1

"1"   "2, 3, 4, 5"

- You should have a pile of four $1 bills on your right. That is how much more you need to save.

70

4 Put the bills back and try it with another goal.

5 For a bigger challenge, write an amount of money between 51¢ and $15.00 on each slip of paper. Make it so there is a mix of dollars and cents. Pick one slip. Look at the amount. Take out the bills you could use to pay that amount.

Imagine the number is $2.15. Let's say you need to pay that amount and you have three $1 bills. How much money would you have left over? Start at $2.15 and use your coins to count up to $3.00.

- $2.15 + 10¢ (dime) = $2.25

- $2.25 + 25¢ (quarter) = $2.50

- $2.50 + 25¢ (quarter) = $2.75

- $2.75 + 25¢ (quarter) = $3.00

- 1 dime + 3 quarters = 85¢

The one dime and three quarters add up to 85¢, which is the amount you have left over.

6 Try this with the amounts written on the six slips.

Why was the skunk so rich?
It had a lot of scents!

Just for Fun!

~ ACTIVITY ~

MONEY COLLECTIONS

A fun and interesting way to save money is to start a coin collection. You can buy special books or cases to keep coins in or make your own.

1 Take a close look at all the coins you have. Which ones would make a good collection? Some of them could be valuable! Some Wisconsin state quarters have an extra leaf on the corn stalk. This makes them rare. If you have a half dollar dated from 1964 or before, it is 90 percent silver! Here are some other ideas for collections:

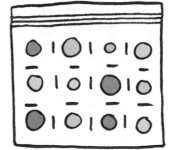

- The 50 different state quarters;
- A coin for each year of your life;
- Special coins such as the four special pennies made in 2009 or the four special nickels made in 2004 and 2005;
- Presidential dollars; and
- Coins from other countries.

2 To keep your coin collection together, put the coins in a plastic zippered bag. Move them around so they are not touching each other. Then use the stapler to staple around each coin.

Bitcoins are a new kind of money that is only online. They are not issued by a government and are not accepted everywhere. What is one way you can use bitcoins? To pay for your trip into space on *Virgin Galactic*.

KNOW YOUR DOUGH

Money is fun to study, save, and spend. And it's changing all the time. Europe is a good example of how much money can change. There are more than 50 countries in Europe. They all used to have their own kind of money. France had francs. Italy had lire. Spain had pesetas.

In the 1960s, some of these countries started planning how to make it easier for people to work, shop, and travel around Europe. They talked about making a new kind of money that would be used in all of their countries. It took a lot of work, but in 1999 the European Union was formed. The euro became the new currency for 14 countries.

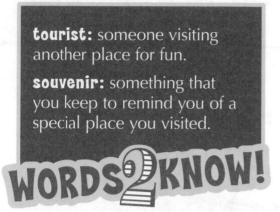

tourist: someone visiting another place for fun.

souvenir: something that you keep to remind you of a special place you visited.

WORDS2KNOW!

What did these countries do with their old money? For a while, banks accepted the old money and traded it for the new kind. Most of the old coins and bills were destroyed. Some people used the old coins to make bracelets and necklaces. **Tourists** love to keep the old coins and bills as **souvenirs** of their trips.

BRITISH POUNDS

When the United States began making its money in 1792, it wanted an easier system than what was used in England at the time. The main currency in England was the pound, which was divided into 20 parts, called shillings. This is just like our nickel, right? But then each shilling was divided into 12 parts, called pence, or one penny. Each penny was divided into four parts, called farthings.

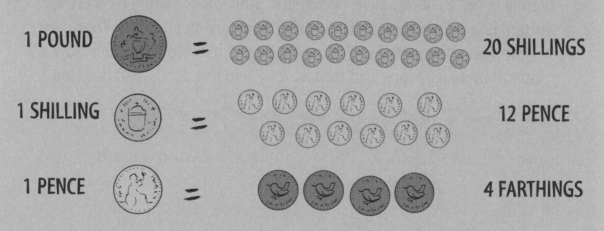

1 POUND = 20 SHILLINGS

1 SHILLING = 12 PENCE

1 PENCE = 4 FARTHINGS

The decimal system was so much easier to follow that by the 1970s nearly all countries around the world had adopted it. The British still use pounds and pence (not euros), but now their system is much simpler. There are 100 pence to the pound.

Today, some people use **virtual** currency that they never see or touch. Virtual currency is traded through plastic cards, computers, and smart phones.

virtual: something that exists on a computer.

WORDS 2 KNOW!

ALL VIRTUAL

Some people think that soon there will be only virtual money. What's so great about virtual money? It can be easier for people who cannot see, because a computer can talk to them about their money. And virtual money will not fall out of your pocket. Virtual money can be the same, everywhere in the world.

Can you think of some problems people might have with virtual money? What if a family doesn't have a computer or smart phone? Will family members be able to have virtual money? Virtual money is a new thing. It will be fascinating to see what happens with currency in the future!

Look at lots of different coins and bills, noticing their shapes, colors, and sizes. Imagine that you no longer needed this money to buy things. How else could you use those pieces of paper and metal circles you have in your bank? You might be surprised. Have some fun with money with these projects!

A 1909 penny was sent to Mars in 2012 with *Curiosity*, a Mars rover. The penny is used to help NASA engineers make sure the rover's camera is working.

KNOW YOUR DOUGH

PS

You can see a picture of the penny covered in Mars dust.

PENNY PICTURE

Look carefully at all of your pennies. Are they all the same color? Although they start as the same shiny, copper color, that color can change over time. You can learn how to clean them in the next activity. Here you can use both shiny and stained pennies to make a picture.

SUPPLIES

$ pennies, old and new

$ sturdy cardboard

$ crayons

$ glue

1 Sort your pennies by color into at least three different piles: very dark brown, medium brown, and bright reddish copper. More piles are even better.

2 Think about a picture you can make with the different colors. Use each pile to make a different shape. The bright ones make a great sun, star, lake, or lightning! The medium ones are good for houses, animals, and autumn leaves. The very dark ones work well for mountains, shadows, and tree trunks.

3 Draw a picture on the cardboard using crayons. Include the coin shapes you made above.

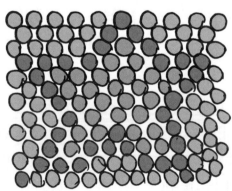

4 Glue the pennies onto the cardboard.

5 Count how much your art is worth in pennies.

TRY THIS! Use other coins—nickels, dimes, quarters, and dollars—in a picture. Or look at a photograph and see if you can recreate it using just your piles of pennies!

CLEAN YOUR COINS

Even if they are used almost every day, coins can last for about 30 years. During that time, they can get very dirty. Just as the U.S. Mint gives coins a bath before they are pressed, you can give your dirty coins a bath too!

SUPPLIES

- $ dirty coins
- $ plastic bottle with wide mouth and cap
- $ sand
- $ water
- $ liquid soap
- $ ketchup
- $ vinegar or lemon juice
- $ table salt
- $ baking soda

1 Put the dirty coins in the bottle.

2 Add about ¼ cup (59 milliliters) of sand, 1 cup (237 milliliters) of water, and a little bit of soap.

3 Put the lid on the bottle and shake hard. Let the bottle sit for a few minutes, then shake again. Repeat this several times.

4 Remove the coins and rinse with clean water.

5 To make pennies shiny, rub them with ketchup or vinegar and salt. Be sure to rinse them off after cleaning them. If they look more pink than copper, rub on a little baking soda.

KNOW YOUR DOUGH

There is a picture of President Abraham Lincoln made with Lincoln pennies on display in his boyhood home in Kentucky!

WHAT'S HAPPENING? Why do you add sand to your water and soap? What does the sand do to the coins?

~ ACTIVITY ~
POP THE DIME

There is air pushing on you all the time. Most of the time you don't notice it. But it can be enough to pop a dime!

SUPPLIES

$ dime (or penny)

$ bottle with opening smaller than the coin

$ bowl of ice cold water

1 Put the coin and the top of the bottle in the bowl of ice water. Or you can put the bottle in a freezer for a few minutes.

2 Put the wet coin on top of the bottle opening. You want the coin to be wet so it makes a seal that doesn't let any air out.

3 Wrap your hands around the bottle. This will help it warm up faster. Watch the coin very carefully.

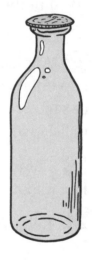

WHAT'S HAPPENING? As the air in the bottle warms up, it expands. As that air takes up more room, it pushes against the coin and makes it pop up a little bit. What do you think would happen if you put the cold bottle in hot water? Could you do a coin toss this way?

COSTLY PENNIES

Today, each penny costs the U.S. Mint more than two cents to make. Why do you think we still have pennies if they cost more to make than they're worth? To save money on making the money, the U.S. government would like to stop issuing pennies and $1 bills. The banks in Australia stopped issuing pennies in 1966 and $1 bills in 1984. The banks in Canada stopped issuing $1 bills in 1987 and pennies in 2013.

CLIP FLIP

SUPPLIES

$ dollar bill
$ 2 paper clips

Can you make two paper clips jump through the air and clip together? You can if you use a dollar bill!

1 Fold the dollar bill into three equal but loose sections. It should look like an S.

2 Clip one end of the bill to the fold closest to it. The paper clip should only go over two layers.

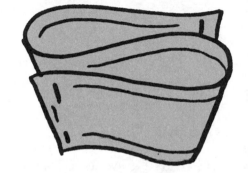

3 Clip the other end of the bill to the fold closest to it. The paper clip should only go over two layers. Both paper clips should be on the top edge of the bill.

4 Grab one end of the bill with one hand and the other end of the bill with the other hand. Pull your hands apart quickly.

5 The paper clips will fly up and come down hooked together!

TRY THIS! What happens if you pull slowly? Or try it with three paper clips? Try putting one paper clip at the top of the bill and the other at the bottom. Try adding a rubber band to one paper clip. What happens if you add more folds?

FLIP A NICKEL

Have you ever had trouble choosing between two things? Sometimes people make a choice by flipping a coin. The heads side of the coin is for one choice, the tails side is for the other. Is that a fair way to choose? Find out!

SUPPLIES

$ nickel or other coin

$ Money Matters Journal

$ pencil

1 Think of two things you like equally, such as sugar cookies and chocolate chip cookies. Think of each side of the coin as a different choice. If heads is sugar cookies, then tails would be chocolate chip.

2 Make a loose fist with one hand with your pinky at the bottom and your thumb resting against the inside of your index finger.

3 Balance the coin over your thumb on your index finger.

4 Quickly flick your thumb up so the coin flies into the air.

There is a legend that the first U.S. nickels were made from President George Washington's melted silverware!

KNOW YOUR DOUGH

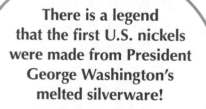

5 When the coin lands, look at which side you can see. What's your decision?

TRY THIS! For extra fun, record the results of your flip in your Money Matters Journal in a chart like the one below. Flip the coin 10 times and record the results.

	HEADS	TAILS
FLIP 1	✔	
FLIP 2	✔	
FLIP 3		✔
FLIP 4		✔
FLIP 5	✔	
FLIP 6	✔	
FLIP 7	✔	
FLIP 8		✔
FLIP 9		✔
FLIP 10	✔	

Do you get heads or tails more often? Does it make a difference if you start with the heads up on your thumb? You can put your results in the Money Math section.

LET'S FLIP FOR IT!

People have flipped a coin to make many important decisions.

* Orville and Wilbur Wright were the first brothers to build a plane that could fly. Wilbur won the coin toss and became the first one to fly their plane.

* When people were starting a new town in Oregon, they used a coin toss to decide its name, Portland.

* People use a coin toss to decide which team gets the football first in the Super Bowl.

QUARTER BUMP

What happens when you line up quarters and act as if they are bumper cars? Try it and find out!

1 Line up three quarters on a table along the side of a ruler. The quarters should be touching.

2 Gently press one finger on the middle quarter.

3 With your other hand, slide another quarter away from the line, then slide it quickly and firmly into the quarter you are holding.

4 Watch what happens to the quarter on the other side! Record how far it moves.

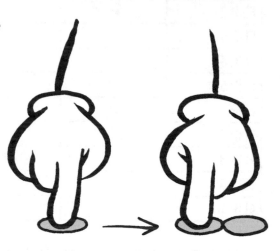

5 Add another quarter to the end of the line to make four quarters in a row.

6 Gently press one finger on one of the quarters in the middle. Slide an end quarter away from and then quickly into the line.

7 Does the far quarter move as far as it did the first time? What do you predict will happen if you add another quarter?

WHAT'S HAPPENING? When you have three or more things in a line, the middle one can't move as freely as the ones on each end. As you move one away and slide it toward the others, you give the middle quarter more energy. When the moving quarter hits the middle one, the extra energy goes into the middle quarter. That energy then goes through the middle quarter and into the third one, which has the room to move. This is called a transfer of energy.

Soldiers during the American Revolution didn't have any place to spend their money. They also didn't have enough warm clothing. Some of them put their paper money around their shins in their boots to help keep them warm. This was how banknotes got the nickname "shinplasters."

KNOW YOUR DOUGH

WHICH QUARTER IS WHICH?

Quarter is a word that can be used for many different things. Any time you divide something into four equal parts, each part is called a quarter. There are:

- ✳ four quarters in a dollar
- ✳ four quarters in a football game
- ✳ four quarts of milk in a gallon

Fifteen minutes equals a quarter of an hour. Can you think of other things that can be divided into four?

EXPLORE MONEY MAD LIB

Fill in the blanks using as many glossary words as you can. You'll end up with a silly story that will change the way you think about money!

noun: a person, place, or thing.
plural noun: more than one person, place, or thing.
adjective: a word that describes a noun.
verb: an action word.
adverb: a word that describes a verb.

_____'s Crazy Cash
<small>YOUR NAME</small>

_____ had _____ _____ in _____ coat pockets. "I am so _____!"
<small>YOUR NAME ⸱ NUMBER ⸱ TYPE OF CURRENCY ⸱ NUMBER ⸱ EMOTION</small>
said _____. I am going to the _____ to _____ a _____. I have been
<small>YOUR NAME ⸱ NOUN ⸱ VERB ⸱ NOUN</small>
_____ for _____ _____. Now I can _____ what I want.
<small>VERB ENDING WITH "ING" ⸱ NUMBER ⸱ PLURAL LENGTH OF TIME ⸱ VERB</small>

_____ _____ to the _____. The _____ was closed! "Oh, no!"
<small>YOUR NAME ⸱ VERB ENDING WITH "ED" ⸱ NOUN ⸱ NOUN</small>
said _____. What am I going to _____?
<small>YOUR NAME ⸱ VERB</small>

_____ _____ by. "Hi, _____. What is wrong?"
<small>NAME OF A FRIEND ⸱ VERB ⸱ YOUR NAME</small>

"I was going to _____ a _____ with my _____ _____ but the _____ is
<small>VERB ⸱ NOUN ⸱ NUMBER ⸱ TYPE OF CURRENCY ⸱ NOUN</small>
closed!"

"Don't worry," said _____. "It is just a _____. You can _____ _____
<small>FRIEND'S NAME AGAIN ⸱ PHRASE ⸱ VERB ⸱ NUMBER</small>
_____ to me. I will keep it _____."
<small>TYPE OF CURRENCY ⸱ ADJECTIVE</small>

_____ thought about it. "That's a _____ idea! I think I will _____ my _____
<small>YOUR NAME ⸱ ADJECTIVE ⸱ VERB ⸱ NUMBER</small>
_____ instead." And that is just what _____ did.
<small>TYPE OF CURRENCY ⸱ YOUR NAME</small>

A

account: a record of the money put in or taken out of a bank.

allowance: a small amount of money given each week or month.

B

bank: a place where money is kept.

banknote: a piece of paper money, also called a bill.

barter: to make an even trade of things that are not alike.

BCE: put after a date, BCE stands for Before Common Era and counts years down to zero. CE stands for Common Era and counts years up from zero. The year this book was published is 2014 CE.

bill: a piece of paper money.

budget: a plan for using money.

buy: to use money to get something you want.

C

cent: the smallest unit in United States money.

change: the extra money given back when something is bought with a larger coin or bill than is needed.

coin: a flat piece of metal stamped with its value as money.

counterfeit: a fake copy made to cheat people.

culture: a group of people and their beliefs and way of life.

currency: the system of money produced by a government in a country.

customer: a person or company that buys goods or services.

D

decimal system: a number system based on units of 10.

deposit: when money is added to a bank account.

digit: a number.

dime: a very small, silver-colored U.S. coin worth 10 cents.

dissolve: to mix with a liquid and become part of the liquid.

dollar: a coin that is gold or silver colored, or a paper banknote worth 100 cents.

dollar: a unit equal to 100 cents in United States money.

donate: to give something, such as money, food, or clothing, to help others.

E

earn: to get something in return for doing work.

etch: to make a pattern or design on a hard material by scratching or burning into the material's surface.

exchange rate: the difference in value between money in one country and money in another country.

exchange: to trade one thing for another.

fee: a charge for a service.

Founding Father: an important person in the founding of the United States.

future: a time that has not happened yet.

goods: things for sale or to use.

half dollar: a large, silver-colored U.S. coin worth 50 cents.

image: a picture.

income: money that comes in from work, an allowance, or an investment.

interest: the fee charged or paid for the use of money.

invest: to let someone else use your money with the possibility of getting more money back. What you invest in is called an investment.

loan: an amount of money that is borrowed and has to be paid back.

medium of exchange: one item used in all trades.

merchant: someone who buys and sells goods for a profit.

money: something used to pay for things, including paying people for their work.

motto: a sentence or phrase that describes a rule or suggests the use or nature of something.

nickel: a silver-colored U.S. coin worth five cents.

obverse: the front or face of a coin.

official: when something is named or approved by the government or someone who is in charge.

P

penny: a copper-colored U.S. coin worth one cent.

preserve: to save food in a way that it won't spoil, so it can be eaten later.

profit: the money made by a business after paying all the costs of the business.

Q

quarter: a medium-sized, silver-colored U.S. coin worth 25 cents.

R

receipt: written proof that goods or money have been given.

regret: to feel sad or sorry about something you did.

reverse: the back or tail of a coin.

risky: an investment that might lose value.

S

service: work done by one person for another person.

slang: a different word for something, used mostly in speech.

souvenir: something that you keep to remind you of a special place you visited.

standard of value: an agreement on how much something is worth in a country's medium of exchange.

stock market: a real and virtual place where people buy and sell their investment loans in different companies.

T

temple: a building used as a place of religion.

token: a round piece of metal or plastic that looks like a coin. It is used in place of a coin in some machines.

tourist: someone visiting another place for fun.

trade: to exchange one thing for something else.

transaction: a deposit to an account or a withdrawal from an account.

treaty: an agreement between two or more countries.

V

value: the price or cost of something, what it is worth.

virtual: something that exists on a computer.

W

withdrawal: when money is taken out of a bank account.

BOOKS

Around the World with Money, Tim Clifford, Rourke Publishing Group, 2008

The Dollar Bill in Translation: What It Really Means, Christopher Forest, Capstone, 2009

Follow the Money, Loreen Leedy, Holiday House, 2003

The Kids Guide to Money Cent$, Keltie Thomas, Kids Can Press, 2004

Money, Money, Money: Where It Comes From, How to Save It, Spend It, Make It, Eve Drobot, Maple Tree Press, 2004

National Geographic Kids Everything Money: A Wealth of Facts, Photos, and Fun! Kathy Furgang, National Geographic Children's Books, 2013

WEBSITES

Schoolhouse Rock video about bartering:
www.youtube.com/watch?v=wHY5cdExNa8

More information about the history and making of U.S. coins: *www.usmint.gov*

More information about the history and making of U.S. bills: *bep.gov*

An up-close look at the security features of U.S. bills:
www.secretservice.gov/KnowYourMoneyApril08.pdf

See a virtual tour of the U.S. Mint at:
www.usmint.gov/mint_tours/?action=vtShell

More information about U.S. banking:
www.federalreserveeducation.org/about-the-fed/structure-and-functions/financial-services/fun_facts.cfm

More information about coin collecting:
coins.about.com/od/uscoins/tp/errorvarieties.htm
www.usmint.gov/kids/campCoin/collectorsWorkshop/coinCourse/04.cfm

A list of all the currencies for countries around the world:
fx.sauder.ubc.ca/currency_table.html

PRIMARY SOURCE QR CODES

page 30:
www.youtube.com/watch?v=YcXcH6yL8p8

page 48:
www.xe.com/currencycharts/

page 75:
www.collectspace.com/news/news-101513a.html

Visit NomadPress.net to check out some great places to visit and learn even more about money!

INDEX

A

activities
Bank Register, 54–55
Barter Chart, 10–11
Big Numbers, 56–59
Clean Your Coins, 77
Clip Flip, 79
Coin Chart, 24–25
Coin Testing, 27
Counting Challenge, 42–43
Count Up Change, 70–71
Dollar Detective, 40–41
Double Delight, 68–69
Etch Your Sketch, 44
Explore Money Mad Lib, 84
Flip a Nickel, 80–81
Make a Bank, 53
Money Collections, 72
My Money Matters Journal, 9
Paper Money, 37–39
Penny Picture, 76
Pockets Plan, 66–67
Pop the Dime, 78
Quarter Bump, 82–83
Super Sorting, 26
Trading Up, 52
Understanding Place Value, 50–51
Australian money, 78

B

banks (*see also* Federal Reserve)
accounts with, 46–49, 54–55, 61, 65
checks from, 49
currency exchange by, 48, 49
definition of, 8, 45
deposits into, 46, 49, 54–55, 65
history of, 45–48
interest charged/paid by, 48, 61, 65
loans from, 48, 51, 65
money earned by, 46, 47–48
old money traded to, 74
saving money in, 61, 63
withdrawals from, 46, 49, 54–55
bartering, iv, 2–3, 7, 10–11
"Benjamins" terminology, 51
bills
basic features of, 31–32
counterfeit, 7, 31, 39, 40
durability of, 33–35, 37–39
elements included on, 32–35, 40–41
fifty dollar, 35
five dollar, 34, 40–41
history of first, v, 7, 28–30
large denomination, 41
material used for, 31, 37–39, 41
one dollar, 33, 36, 40–41, 78
one hundred dollar, 35, 51
printing of, 30, 31–32, 44
Roman numerals on, 36
serial numbers on, 31, 32, 47
ten dollar, 34
twenty dollar, 35
two dollar, 34
U.S., v, 30–36 (*see also* specific bills)
valuation of, 30, 32–33, 41, 42–43
bitcoins, iv, 7, 72
borrowing money, 48, 51, 65, 69
British money, 74
"buck" terminology, 29
budgets, 8, 61, 66–67, 70
buried or hidden money, 45, 53

C

Canadian money, 49, 78
checks/checking accounts, 49
Chinese money, iv–v, 6, 13, 28–30
coins
bankers receiving, 45–46 (*see also* banks)
buried, 45, 47
collecting, 21, 72
dimes as, 19–20
flipping, 80–81
half-dollars as, 22
heaviness of, 7, 28–29
history of first, iv–v, 6–7, 12–14
metal for, iv–v, 6, 17, 18, 19, 20, 22, 23, 27, 28, 30, 47, 80
nickels as, 17–18, 80
one dollar coins as, 13, 19, 23
pennies as, 16–17, 76, 78
quarters as, 20–21, 82–83
tokens and, 20
U.S., v, 14–23, 77–78 (*see also* specific coins)
valuation of, 14–15, 16, 18, 20, 21, 22, 23, 24
collecting money, 21, 72
copper, iv, 17, 18, 19, 20, 22, 23
counterfeit money, 7, 31, 39, 40
credit cards, 47, 75
currency exchange, 48, 49

D

dimes, 19–20
donating money, 8, 60, 64, 68–69

E

earning money, 5, 46, 47–48, 60, 64–65
European money, iv, v, 30, 73–74

F

Federal Reserve, 30, 41
fifty dollar bills, 35
five dollar bills, 34, 40–41

flipping coins, 80–81
Franklin, Benjamin, 35, 51
fun with money, 73–84

G

gold, v, 6, 23, 47
Grant, Ulysses S., 35
"greenback" terminology, 30

H

half dollars, 22
Hamilton, Alexander, 34

I

interest, 48, 61, 65, 69
investing money, 8, 60,
  64–65, 69
iron, 6, 27

J

Jackson, Andrew, 35
Jefferson, Thomas, 18, 34

K

Kennedy, John, 22

L

Lewis and Clark expedition,
  18, 19
Lincoln, Abraham, 17, 34, 77
loans, 48, 51, 65, 69
Lydian money, v, 6, 12–13

M

MacDonald, Kyle, 2
managing money, 8, 60–72
manganese, 23
metal money, iv–v, 5, 6–7,
  12–23, 27, 28, 30, 47, 80
  (see also coins)
money
  banks and, 8, 45–59, 61,
    63, 65, 74
  bartering instead of, iv, 2–3,
    7, 10–11
  bills as, v, 7, 28–44, 47,
    51, 78

borrowing, 48, 51, 65, 69
budgeting, 8, 61, 66–67, 70
buried or hidden, 45, 47, 53
coins as, iv–v, 6–7, 12–27,
  28–29, 30, 45–46, 47, 72,
  76–78, 80–83
collecting, 21, 72
counterfeit, 7, 31, 39, 40
currency exchange of, 48, 49
definition and description
  of, 1, 3
donating or sharing, 8, 60,
  64, 68–69
earning, 5, 46, 47–48, 60,
  64–65
fun with, 73–84
history of first, iv–v, 3–7,
  12–14, 28–30
investing, 8, 60, 64–65, 69
saving, 8, 60, 61, 63
slang for, 29, 30, 51, 83
spending, 8, 60, 61–63
timeline of, iv–v
using or managing, 8,
  60–72
valuation of (see valuation)
virtual, iv, 7, 72, 75

N

nickel (metal), 18, 19, 20,
  22, 23
nickels, 17–18, 80

O

one dollar bills, 33, 36,
  40–41, 78
one dollar coins, 13, 19, 23
one hundred dollar bills,
  35, 51

P

paper money, v, 7, 29–39
  (see also bills)
pennies, 16–17, 76, 78
Polo, Marco, 30

Q

quarters, 20–21, 82–83

R

receipts, v, 7
Roman money, 4, 5
Roosevelt, Franklin D., 19
Russian money, 13

S

Sacagawea, 19, 23
salt, 4, 5
saving money, 8, 60, 61, 63
sharing money, 8, 60, 64,
  68–69
"shinplasters" terminology, 83
silver, 5, 6, 12, 23, 80
Spanish money, 13–14, 21
spending money, 8, 60, 61–63
stocks/stock market, 65, 69
Sumerian money, 5, 12

T

ten dollar bills, 34
timeline of money, iv–v
tokens, 20
trading, iv, 2–3, 7, 10–11, 29
twenty dollar bills, 35
two dollar bills, 34

V

valuation
  big number, 56–59
  of bills, 30, 32–33, 41, 42–43
  of coins, 14–15, 16, 18, 20,
    21, 22, 23, 24
  place value of, 50–52
virtual money, iv, 7, 72, 75

W

Washington, George, 21, 33,
  80

Z

zinc, 17, 23